In the Midst of the Storm

Dorenthea Nemeth

Copyright © 2017 Dorenthea Nemeth

All rights reserved. No part of this publication may be reproduced, stored in a retrieval system, or transmitted, in any form or in any means – by electronic, mechanical, photocopying, recording or otherwise – without prior written permission.

ISBN-13: 978-1451551884
ISBN-10: 1451551886

Unless otherwise indicated, all Scripture quotations are taken from the King James Version of the Bible.

To my babies and my angels,
Albert and Alivia,
that God used to bless me
so that I could endure my storms

Contents

Introduction 1
My Wilderness Experience 5
Don't Quit 16
Midnight Hour 23
The Wait 31
Don't Forget 37
I Never Would've Thought 44
Seasons Change 49
Transformers 53
It's Time To Worship 56
Bonus Chapter 62

Introduction

Peter thought he knew Jesus. Jesus asked him, "Who do you say that I the son of man am?" Peter said, "Thou are the Christ, the Son of the living God." From this verse, it would be fair to say that Peter knew Jesus. But did he *really* know Jesus? He thought he did. After all, he ate with Jesus, fished with Jesus, watched him perform miracles, feed thousands with very little. He raised people from the dead. Peter saw Him heal the lame and the sick. But did he really know Jesus?

Peter's like a lot of us today. We go to church, say a 30-second prayer over our food, and go through the routines of Christianity.

And we say, "Oh yeah, I know Jesus." Yet, we

don't know him anymore than we do our next door neighbor. Oh, that I may know Him!

As we read Luke 22, following Jesus' arrest, Peter denied Jesus three times. After that third time, verse 61 says, "And the Lord turned, and looked upon Peter." And immediately, Peter began to weep. Peter cried a cry of shame and I believe, of repentance. I believe that it was at this time that, when Jesus gave him that *look,* he knew, really knew, that Jesus truly was the Son of God. I believe he thought like Jacob did, "The Lord was in this place, and I knew it not." Oh, that I may Him!

Now, before I go any further, I just want to clarify myself and say that I'm not talking to the ones who are satisfied with the status quo, "Well, I'll just go to church on Sunday, read my Bible for five minutes a week, pray for five minutes, and I'm OK." This book is for those who are willing and ready to go to that next level in God and cry out to Him, "Lord, I want to know you!"

We all make mistakes. Proverbs 24:16 says, "…for though a righteous man falls seven times, he rises again…" (NIV) But we must be very careful that we don't play with God. He tells us in Revelation to be either hot or cold. If you're lukewarm, He said He'll spew you out of His mouth.

Introduction

Though Peter denied Jesus, not once, not twice, but three times, it didn't cancel the plan and destiny that God had for his life. Earlier Jesus told Peter in Matthew 16:18, "And I say also unto thee, That thou art Peter, and upon this rock I will build my church; and the gates of hell shall not prevail against it." In other words Jesus tells Peter that he is the rock that he will build his church on. He says that upon this rock, not even the gates of hell will be able to stand against the church. Later in the New Testament, we find Peter performing the same miracles that Jesus did. We fall down, but we get back up again! The Lord wants you to know that He's about to make some rough places plain and smooth.

I don't know about you, but I'm tired of settling for scraps. Let's take the Prodigal Son, for instance. He had it going on, everything he needed was there for the asking. But that wasn't enough for him, so he wanted his inheritance so he could leave the nest and enjoy the 'good' life. Well, needless to say, he lost it doing things 'his way'. He later had to get a job and the only one he could find was a job as a cleaner of pigpens. Even the pigs were eating better than him. He finally came to himself, because he realized that eating pig slop wasn't his nature.

We want everything that life has to offer, but we first must be willing to change. God wants to change your nature. Your soul is worth far more than houses, money, etc. Once you let Him change you and mold you, everything else will fall into place. We all know Matthew 6:33, "But seek ye first the kingdom of God, and his righteousness; and all these things shall be added unto you." God wants abundant life for you. You don't have to settle for pig slop. God has more for you. He wants to give you blessings that will blow your mind. You're one prayer away from your deliverance. You're one praise away from your breakthrough. The very thing that the devil meant to destroy you, God's going to use it as the key to unlock the door to your destiny. You will reap if you faint not.

My Wilderness Experience

Wherefore seeing we also are compassed about with so great a cloud of witnesses, let us lay aside every weight, and the sin which doth so easily beset us, and let us run with patience the race that is set before us.

(Hebrews 12:1)

You must get rid of everything that slows you down, especially the sin that just won't let go. Have you ever found yourself committing the same sin over and over again, even though you vowed you weren't going to do it again? That's because it's a stronghold. A stronghold has such a strong hold on you, it's like a tick or a leech draining the life out of you.

When you don't learn how to conquer those things that control you, they become strongholds. It can be pride, worry, depression, smoking, drinking, cursing, gossiping, etc. These are some strongholds in our lives that hold us back, that keep us from receiving the fullness of God's blessings. So, in order to receive the promises of God and get your prayers answered you have to humble yourself. Second Chronicles 7:14 says, "If my people, which are called by my name, shall *humble* themselves, and pray, and seek my face, and turn from their wicked ways; then will I hear from heaven, and will forgive their sin, and will heal their land." God gives us the chance to humble ourselves; to say no to our flesh; to say no to temptation and sin. If we fail in doing this, God will do it for us. It's better if you humble yourself, than for God to humble you.

First, you have to humble yourself and realize that you are nothing, and can do nothing, without Him. Then, it says, "…pray, and seek my face, and turn from your wicked ways…" There's a price to pay, and the question you have to ask yourself, "Am I willing to pay the price?" How bad do you want it?

My husband, Albert, and I were married on March 13, 1993. Everything was wonderful— until. The signs were there that Albert really wasn't saved before we got married. Once I found a cigarette lighter in his car and I questioned him about it. He just acted like it was nothing, took it out of my hand and threw it out of the window. I was so naïve that I didn't question him about it anymore. You see, I was this girl who grew up in church all my life. I didn't associate with marijuana smokers, but unbeknownst to me, Albert was one. He had accepted the Lord and was baptized and filled with the Holy Spirit. However, he only knew God in his head, not his heart. About a year after our wedding, he backslid. Six months after that, in August 1994, my "wilderness" experience began.

Our beautiful apartment with its new furniture was destroyed by fire. Albert was in jail, so I went to stay with my parents. Three days later, between 2:30 a.m. and 4:30 a.m., a police officer knocked on my parents' door to inform me that my car was set on fire in the middle of a corn field, about 75-90 miles from where my parents live. I felt like Job. Albert had turned his back on God and I had lost everything I had.

Albert got out of jail. We got back together and joined the most wonderful church in Toledo. Things were looking up again. We moved into an apartment with an old table, two chairs, and a $200 brass bed that was never used. Albert was working at the church as a maintenance man and I was a billing clerk for a chiropractic company. A year later I gave birth to a healthy 8lb 12oz baby boy. Twenty-two months later, I gave birth to our beautiful daughter. We moved into a house and I became a homemaker. Albert got another job with insurance benefits and making more money. Things couldn't be better—until.

He got laid off. A few weeks later he got an even higher paying job working for the union. However, he still had a void in his life. His closeness with the Lord began to dwindle, again. And he started smoking marijuana, again. I didn't know it until much later because he never did it around me.

I had finally gotten to the point that I was tired of living a *less than* life. Deep down inside, I knew that God had more for me and more for my marriage. I wanted what God had for me—not just life, but ABUNDANT life. So, one night while I was sitting in the tub, crying, I released Albert to the Lord and asked Him to do whatever He had to do to bring him back to Him.

Be careful about what you pray for, because you just might get it. A few weeks later, there was a knock on the door. It was a police detective, a sergeant and two police officers at my door with a search warrant. Albert was sitting in one of the four police cars sitting in our driveway with handcuffs on. He had been arrested. When they came in the house looking for evidence, God gave me total peace. The detective asked me why I was so calm and serene, and not crying or going into a panic. I told him that my parents took me to church all my life and I have a relationship with God. Then he said, "You're saying that it's God that gives you this…" He didn't know what to call it, but I said, "peace". The world doesn't even know about the peace that only God can give. Philippians 4:6-7 says, "Be careful for nothing; but in everything by prayer and supplication with thanksgiving let your requests be made known unto God. And the peace of God, which passes all understanding, shall keep your hearts and minds through Christ Jesus." God is saying, "Don't worry about anything. But, instead, pray about everything. And you will have peace."

Today, Albert is sitting in prison serving a 16-year sentence. But it's not as bad as it sounds. He's ministering to other inmates. Some inmates he doesn't even know write him notes, asking him questions about the Bible. He knows more about the Word now than I do, and he's teaching a Bible class. He's so dogmatic about the Word, and in obeying every word in it. He not only knows the Lord in his head now, but he finally has Him in his heart. But this was the price we had to pay.

We all will encounter a "wilderness experience" in our lives at one point or another. But that's when you must remember His Word.

In Jeremiah 29:11, He says that His "plans for you are for good and not evil; to give you a future and a hope." Know that He is your glory and the lifter of your head. He'll be your peace and joy in the midst of the storm. He'll be your oasis in a dry desert. God is enlarging me and Albert, even while we're in the wilderness. He's pouring on us His power and anointing. God will use your wilderness to turn the key that will open the door to your destination. This is not the time or the place to give up. You will reap if you faint not. The Bible tells us to "count it ALL joy." When you are weak, then you're strong. It's during the hard times that we gain the most strength. God will allow your test to become a testimony so that your ministry will be more effective. People don't want to hear anybody who's never been through anything. But once you've gone through a test or trial, you can tell someone else, "What you're going through, I've already been there and He'll bring you out just like he brought me out." The Bible says, "comfort others with the comfort wherewith we ourselves have been comforted of God…"

Don't focus on the problem, but focus on the provider because He's the only one who can bring you through. I can't remember the countless times that the Lord provided for and blessed me. When Albert first became incarcerated, my church family blessed me in ways unexpected. Some gave me money or bought groceries for me and my children. One church brother with his own family even came to get my children for a couple of hours so that I could have some time to myself, and he filled my car with gas a few times. Once, someone at the church who I didn't even know gave me money. One morning, I woke up to a bag of clothes sitting on my porch. Once I prayed for the money to get my carpet cleaned. About five minutes after I prayed, I received a phone call from my mother telling me that one of my uncles gave her $500.00 to give to me. One time I had a $90.00 bill that was past due. I didn't want to use my credit card, so I prayed and asked the Lord to bless me with the money. The next day, someone blessed me with a check for $100.00.

Before Albert's arrest, unbeknownst to me, he took out a loan using my car as collateral. I found out about it after his arrest and didn't have the money to pay off the loan, so the car was due to be taken, leaving me without transportation. One Wednesday night while I was at church, one of the brothers asked me how I was doing. I'm not one to talk about my personal business, but for some reason I told him about my car being taken. Later that week, he called me and said that the church had been a great blessing to him and his family during the birth of his last child who was facing death. So, he and his wife wanted to be a blessing to someone else. And I'll never forget what he said on the phone next, "And that just happens to be you, girlfriend." Now, mind you, this was a Caucasian brother calling me 'girlfriend'. So, he and his wife blessed me with $1,000.00.

Others also gave me money, and on top of that, another brother went to look for a car for me and all I had to do was pay for it. God did a quick work. So when the bank came to pick up the other car, I didn't have to worry or go into a panic, because the need had already been met! Believe me when I say that God will supply ALL your needs. He will truly make a way out of no way. God has proven Himself to me over and over again, and He will do the same thing for you. God is enlarging His people with greater faith, greater power, greater anointing.

Each of us has a calling according to God's purpose, to be manifested in His timing. But at the time you're going through a storm, things look hopeless. When Albert called me on the day of his sentencing and gave me the news, a spirit of depression came on me. It was a feeling of despair and hopelessness. It was something I had never felt in my whole life. It was the worst feeling. When it feels like all hell has come against you, pray, cry out to God. Psalm 34:6 says, "This poor man cried, and the LORD heard him, and saved him out of all his troubles." Whatever you need, whether it's healing, deliverance, a financial blessing or miracle, trust in God and wait on Him. Whatever you do, don't give up. If you can't fly, run; if you can't run, walk; if you can't walk, then crawl. The race is not given to the swift; nor the battle to the strong, but to him that endures to the end.

My friends and family were my angels during the worst time of my life. When you obey and worship God, you will touch Him in such a way that He will send His angels to your aid, to bless you and cover you.

One night when I was trying to fall asleep, I saw myself in the spirit, hanging on a cross. It blew me away. I started thinking about the verse that says, "I am crucified with Christ, and it is no longer I that live, but Christ that lives in me." The Lord let me know that even though I didn't have to die the kind of death he did, when Albert was sentenced for so many years, I felt hopeless, like part of me died. I cried for three days. Jesus was in the tomb for three days, but Praise God, on that third day, He rose again.

The devil thought he had me, but my spirit came back to life again. Now, I'm the Minister of Music and a Sunday School teacher at my church, and I'm giving the devil a black eye with my praise. The Lord gave me fresh oil and new wine. He gave me a new outlook, a new attitude, fresh power, and fresh anointing. But it cost me something.

Sometimes it feels like all hell has broken loose, problem after problem. But look up, your redemption, your deliverance is already here. Sometimes we try to do things our way and we end up wearing ourselves out, when all God wants us to do is 'look up.' Look to Him. Trust Him to bring you out and help you. David said, "I will lift my eyes unto the hills from whence cometh my help, my help comes from the Lord." Don't look to the left or to the right. Look up! Albert and I are closer today and more in love with each other than the day we married. We're best friends now. God has put such strength and character in us. Our strengths, the reasons we fell in love in the first place, have been enhanced and brought to a whole new level, in a way that wouldn't have happened without the storm. I heard someone say in a movie, "Crouching Tiger and Hidden Dragon", "To be strong and supple is the secret to overcoming the storm." Through your storm, He will make you strong and supple, able to bend under pressure without breaking.

Don't Quit

Consider it pure joy, my brothers, whenever you face trials of many kinds, because you know that the testing of your faith develops perseverance. Perseverance must finish its work so that you may be mature and complete, not lacking anything."

(James 1:2- 4 NIV)

In Matthew 9:27-30, Jesus healed two blind men. Notice that Jesus didn't ask them, "How much money do you have in your checking account?" "What sin did you commit to bring blindness on yourself?" He simply asked them, "Do you believe?"

The enemy can have you thinking, "You'll never be able to afford that car or a new home."

"You've been too bad." We've put God in a box, like He can't do more than what our income allows. Yet the Bible says, "He owns the cattle on a thousand hills." It says, "The earth is the Lord's and the fullness thereof." That means everything that's on the earth, all the houses, all the cars, all the silver, all the gold, all the money, it's all His. It all belongs to Him and since you're an heir of God, which according to Webster's dictionary is 'one who inherits or is entitled to inherit property', then everything that belongs to Him belongs to you.

But the question is, "Do you believe?" When Jesus asked the blind men this question, they said, "Yea, Lord." In other words, "Yes, Lord, we believe." Can we say that when our backs are up against the wall? "Yes, Lord, I believe." Can you truly say that or is there still some doubt in the back of your mind, some worry? Do you believe? Do you trust Him? Is your faith in your money, or is it in God? And it can't be in both because James 1 says when you ask for something, don't waver. Don't be like the waves of the sea. A wave rises, and it falls. We get our hopes up high. Our faith is high. We just heard a good message, and we're like, "Praise God! This is my season! This is my year!"

Then, here comes a large bill; something in the house needs repairing; the car needs repairing;

you lose your job; the unemployment checks are getting ready to run out; your child has turned his back on God; you just got an eviction notice; you or someone you love has just been diagnosed with cancer. Now, what do you do? Keep on walking. Keep believing. Keep resting in God. Keep speaking His Word.

There's so much that God has put inside of you. There's power inside of you. There's anointing inside of you. There's ministry inside of you. There's great faith inside of you. But in order for it to come forth, you can't quit.

Ephesians 3:20, "Now unto him that is able to do exceeding abundantly above all that we ask or think, according to the *power* that worketh in us." You need power. It takes power to trust God. It takes power to give when you're broke. It takes power to save money for a car or a house when all you want to do is spend it. It takes power to praise and worship when all you want to do is cry. It takes power to pray when all you want to do is complain and fuss. It takes power to stay committed when all you want to do is throw in the towel and give up. It takes power to be faithful to a man sentenced to 16 years in prison, and that's exactly what kept me. As of the writing of this book, I have remained celibate for nearly 10 years now. Once, one of my coworkers asked me, "How do you do it?" I told her, "It's God."

He has given me the power to remain faithful to Albert. Was I tempted? Yes. But I was, and still am committed to Albert. And even more so, I'm committed to God. When I said my marriage vows, I meant them.

We all experience challenges and difficult times in our lives when life is simply, well, hard. We need God. And it takes more than just going to church. You don't receive power just by going to church. You receive power in your obedience and in your commitment to the Lord.

Many times the Lord will allow things to test us to get us out of our comfort zone. There are so many blessings that He has for you, but before you can have them, you must first learn to trust Him and know that He knows what's best for you. That's what faith is.

Let us go back to Matthew 9:29, "Then touched he their eyes saying, 'According to your faith, be it unto you.'" He didn't say, "According to your talent…" He didn't say, "According to how much money you make." But He said, "According to your faith." It's done. What you prayed for is a done deal. The whole world is yours for the asking.

You must train yourself to have faith. Faith isn't dependent upon feelings. It isn't in a bunch of stuff, but it's saying like Job said, "Though He slay me, yet will I trust Him."

James 1:2 says, "My brethren, count it all joy when ye fall into divers temptations." In other words, rejoice, even if you have a lot of trouble. You may ask, "How can I rejoice when I'm going through?" Many times when we're being tested, we ask God to remove the problem. Psalm 34:19 says, "Many are the afflictions of the righteous: but the LORD delivers him out of them all." Notice that it doesn't say, "When you have problems, just ask me to take them away and I will." But what it is saying is that your test is only for a season. It's temporary. But you must remember that it's not for nothing.

God doesn't allow you to go through problems for the fun of it. They're to teach you something, to give you wisdom. That's why James later says in verse 5, "If any of you lack wisdom, let him ask of God, that giveth to all men liberally, and upbraids not; and it shall be given him." I heard someone say, when trouble comes, you have two choices. You can either get bitter, or you can get creative. And we've all heard this one, "When you're handed a bowl of lemons (problems), make lemonade." You have a choice. You can let your problems get you down, or you can submit and humble yourself and say, "OK, Lord, what are you trying to tell me? What are you trying to teach me? What are you trying to do in me, through me, and for me? I need wisdom for this situation." Then, get in His Word. When Solomon was young, beginning his kingship, the Lord visited him in a vision and asked him what did he want Him to do for him. All he had to do was ask, and it was his. Solomon asked for wisdom. And the Lord told him, "Because you didn't seek my hand, but you sought my wisdom, I'm going to give you everything else that you could've asked for, but didn't."

Our problem is we're seeking and pursuing the wrong things. We put everything else before God. We give Him the leftovers, but we want the best of everything.

In the book of Nehemiah, we find Nehemiah with the task of rebuilding the wall of Jerusalem. Nehemiah received a letter from his enemies, posing as friends, to coerce him into leaving his work. They were persistent for they sent a letter to him five times asking to meet with him. The devil knows how to make himself appear as an angel of light, but he's really a wolf in sheep's clothing. And that's why it's so important to know the will of God. How do you know His will? By getting in His Word. God's will is His Word understood.

Nehemiah's enemies figured that if they could distract him for just a few minutes—if they could get his focus off of God's will for his life. Then, they could stop the Israelites from regaining their land, dignity and self- respect.

The devil knows that if he can take your focus off of God and what His Word says and promises to you, His child, he then has permission to bring problems in your family, your job, your life; make you depressed and worried about bills, etc. This gives him a foothold and his work is done.

However, when you know what God's word says, you can then stand flat-footed against the enemy and say, "Devil, you are a liar! No matter what, I'm going to praise and worship my God. I am the head and not the tail. My finances are blessed. My spouse and my children are saved. Peace is in my home. By His stripes we are healed. My marriage is blessed…" This is wisdom, not allowing the devil to cause you to take your eyes off the prize. When God is for you, He's more than the world against you.

Wisdom preserves you, keeps you safe, gives you peace and makes you mature. The more word you have, you are better able to make wise decisions. Proverbs 4:8 says, "Exalt her (wisdom), and she shall promote thee: she shall bring thee to honour, when thou dost embrace her."

Midnight Hour

I am come that you might have life and that you might have it more abundantly.

(John 10:10)

Have you ever felt like you're ready for the "next level" because you're no longer satisfied with the norm? God is preparing you because He has put a longing in you for something more. Determine in your mind that from this day on you will be faithful in the small things so that the Lord can release you into the greater things of the kingdom that He has for you. Pray. Don't doubt. Get back what the devil stole. Whatever you're praying for, act like it's going to happen today. And GET READY!!

Stand still and see the salvation of the Lord.

He's ordering your footsteps. One day the Lord said to me, "Don't move. Stay where you're at because I'm getting ready to bless you. Because you have the mind to please me, I'm going to open doors for you that you know not of. I knew your thoughts before you thought them. I want you to stand still. Stop worrying."

There's a song that says, "Late in the midnight hour, God's gonna turn it around; He's gonna work in your favor." When I first thought about 'midnight hour', I thought it meant late at night while I was asleep. Granted, while we're asleep, things are going on in the spirit realm in our favor that we know not of. But not just when we're asleep, but all through the day. At midnight it's very dark and dreary. Spiritually speaking, you can't see any light. You can't see a way out, and you're thinking, "God, if you don't do this, it won't be done." Doubt and fear start to take over. The 'midnight hour' for the children of Israel was when they stood face to face with the Red Sea and Pharaoh and his army behind them. They started complaining, "Moses you brought us here to die. We were better off in Egypt (in bondage)." The 'midnight hour' for Paul & Silas was when they were in a cold dark prison filled with rats, in chains, beaten. But instead of complaining, they sang hymns and spiritual songs. The Bible tells us we're going to have tests, midnight hours. But it's up to us what we do in our midnight hours. Will you complain and question God, "Why me?", or will you praise Him and sing hymns? God is so good because even though the Israelites complained over and over again, He still turned it around and worked in their favor. However, they didn't have peace. They always panicked and worried about this thing or that. You can choose to panic and get anxious. But when you do, you disobey the Word of God. Philippians 4:6 says, "Be careful (anxious; worried) for nothing; but in everything by prayer and supplication with thanksgiving let your requests be made known unto God. And the peace of God, which passes all understanding, shall keep your hearts and minds through Christ Jesus." You won't be like the Israelites, but like Paul & Silas. You will say like Job said, "Though He slay me, yet will I trust Him." Psalms says His thoughts about you are like the grains of sand on the seashore—many, constantly, all day long. Sometimes we ask God for something, and we may not get the answer until just before—at the last minute—'late in the midnight hour'—and God turns it around and works in our favor. Yes, you're going to have some midnight hours, when you can't see a way out. But, the question is, "What will you do in your midnight hour?"

Sometimes we can move before God's timing.

Positions look glamorous, but you're going to have to go through something to have that anointing. High positions look good and they sound good, but the Bible says, my sheep know my voice. You have to know if it's the Holy Ghost or the devil. In 2 Corinthians 12, Paul said that Satan's messenger had come to buffet him. But he rejoiced in his tests, because in his weakness, God was made strong. I believe that we'll never be perfect until we get to heaven, because God allows each of us to have a Satanic messenger to buffet us so that He will get the glory out of our lives. God wants our praise. We were created to praise Him, to lift Him up, to magnify and glorify His name. And whatever it takes to draw us closer to Him, to get our attention, whether good or bad, He's going to do it, because in our weaknesses, God is made strong. He does it because He loves us. His word says in Jeremiah, "I have loved thee with an everlasting love; therefore, with loving-kindness have I drawn thee." He wants to be everything to us—peace, love, joy, wonderful counselor, etc. He wants us to totally depend on him.

The devil wants you to think there's something wrong with you, because as long as he has you thinking that, he knows he has you bound. You have to learn the devil's strategies. Now, for every negative thought that enters your mind, think about a verse in the Word that counteracts that thought. "Resist the devil and he will flee." Revelation says you "overcome by the blood of the lamb and by the word of your testimony." Everything you need, wisdom, power, healing, deliverance, are wrapped up in those two things, the blood of the lamb and the word of your testimony. We have the power to speak blessing or cursing, life or death. There's nothing wrong with you. You are a child of the king. Praise God! You are royal! 1 Peter 2:9, "But ye are a chosen generation, a royal priesthood, an holy nation, a peculiar people: that ye should show forth the praises of him who hath called you out of darkness into his marvelous light." There are going to be times when you will feel uncomfortable and go through tests that don't feel good. God is squeezing life into you. It's all part of the process. You're getting closer and closer to your destiny. Give Him your undivided attention because when your focus is totally on Him, you won't be shaken, no matter the circumstance. Choose to surrender your thoughts, mind, spirit, soul and body to God, and you won't be sorry.

I decree that you are free from anxiety. You have joy unspeakable and full of glory.

You have peace to the fullest. There's nothing that Satan can do to keep you from your blessing. When you're in a storm and there seems to be no way out, trust in God. He's going to bring you out! You are blessed in the test. "God is preparing you to take possession of your position."

In Nehemiah, he received a letter from an enemy posing as a friend (the devil posing as an angel of light). The enemy wanted Nehemiah to take his eyes off the reward, the prize, and fill him with doubt and fear so that he would stop doing what God had called him to do. Much like today, Satan wants you to take your eyes off God and run away with fear. But when God is for you, He's more than the world against you. Nothing else matters. God knows what's best for you. He may not give you what you want, when you want it, or how you want it, but He's always on time. And that's all that matters. *All* things are working together for your good. Speak faith and victory, not defeat.

You have to know the devil's schemes. Sometimes it seems like one bad thing happens, then another and another. Luke 10:19 says, "Behold, I give unto you power to tread on serpents and scorpions, and over all the power of the enemy: and nothing shall by any means hurt you." This is God's word to us and whenever Satan comes after you, hold up that shield of faith and the sword of the spirit and proclaim, "I have power over you devil and nothing shall by any means hurt me!" Use the Word. Jesus did. When he was fasting for 40 days, Satan came to Him at his weakest moment, or so it seemed. Three times the devil tried to tempt him. Three times Jesus fought back with the Word saying, "It is written…"

Sometimes, it seems like you go forward one step, then Satan knocks you back two, but the devil is a liar. With every new level comes new devils. Don't let the enemy get you down. Ephesians 6 tells us to "Be strong in the Lord and in the power of His might…so that you may be able to stand against the wiles of the devil." God has something for you and Satan knows it.

The problem is you don't know the power that's on the inside of you. Power is more than positive thinking, but when you speak the Word of God, your words take on feet and go into places you can't go—the hospital room, the prison cell, your job, your children's school, the courthouse, and yes, even the White House. Proverbs 18:20-21a says, "A man's belly shall be satisfied with the fruit of his mouth; and with the increase of his lips shall he be filled. Death and life are in the power of the tongue." We have special privileges as children of God. When we realize our privileges as heirs of God and joint-heirs with Jesus Christ, we can begin to command things to happen. In Matthew 28:18, Jesus said, "And Jesus came and spake unto them, saying, All power is given unto me in heaven and in earth."

Then, Jesus turned around and gave that same power to us because Luke 10:19 says, "Behold, I give unto you power to tread on serpents and scorpions, and over all the power of the enemy: and nothing shall by any means hurt you." The snake may hiss and the lion may roar, but it can't hurt you.

The Wait

Wait on the LORD: be of good courage, and he shall strengthen thine heart: wait, I say, on the LORD.

(Psalm 27:14)

Sometimes the Lord puts us at a roadblock in our lives, a standstill. When you're at a standstill, you can't move to the left or to the right, but just stand still. The Lord has this blessing for you that's so awesome and perfect, that if you don't stand still and wait on Him, you'll mess it up. The Christian life is falling down and getting back up again. Faith (masculine) plus patience (feminine) produce a baby called joy. The book of James says, "But let patience have her perfect work, that ye may be perfect and entire, wanting nothing." In other words, patience must go the full term, like a woman pregnant with a child.

In order for all the organs to be fully matured, the pregnancy must go its full term of nine months. When you put faith and patience together, you will become pregnant with joy. Just like a baby is born at the appointed time, you will receive the promise that God has promised you at the appointed time. Blessings are going to overtake you and your cup is going to run over. When patience goes the full term, there are no miscarriages; no abortion of your destiny.

When you look at your problem through God's eyes, you will see that you are an overcomer. You are more than a conqueror. Greater is He that's in you than he that's in the world. The Bible says that in this world we will have tribulation, but God says, "Be of good cheer." Cheer up! Chill! You have overcome the world. We serve an awesome God!

Life gets boring sometimes— repetitive; same thing day after day. It was like that even in the Bible. Ten times God had Moses go before Pharaoh to persuade him to let the Israelites go. And God even told him that He was going to harden Pharaoh's heart, but Moses had to do it anyway. Seven times Elijah told his servant to go check and see if he saw a cloud or any sign of rain following the 3½ year drought that Elijah had pronounced in the first place. If I could've read Moses and Elijah's servant's minds, I would say that they were probably thinking, "God, what's up? I'm tired of going back and forth." But they didn't complain. They were obedient. I would say that Moses and Elijah's servant were some patient men. They obeyed and waited. This is what God is calling us to do—obey and wait, obey and wait. Trust God and know that as long as you continue to obey and wait on God, your blessing, your miracle is coming.

At my former church, I used to in the choir. As *praise teams* became more popular, the choir eliminated, and I wasn't asked to continue ministry on the new praise team. After months had passed and I still wasn't singing in ministry, I felt like someone had put a muzzle on my mouth. But during that time when I was no longer singing in the choir, the Lord began to give me songs while I slept, songs that have never been sung. He spoke to my spirit and let me know that even though I was in this dry season of not being able to use my talent, He let me know that He was still with me and that I will sing again. He let me know that His anointing upon me would be great. God said in Isaiah, "I'll give you beauty for ashes, the oil of joy for mourning, the garment of praise for the spirit of heaviness."

There's a short story in Luke 13 about a man

who had a fig tree planted in his yard. One day he told his gardener, "This tree hasn't produced fruit for the past three years. Chop it down for there's no reason letting it live just taking up space in the ground." But the gardener said in verses 8 and 9, "And he answering said unto him, Lord, let it alone this year also, till I shall dig about it, and dung it: And if it bear fruit, well: and if not, then after that thou shalt cut it down." In others words he was saying, "I'll dig around it and put some manure and fertilizer on it to make it grow."

Some of us have gotten complacent. We say, "I'm satisfied right where I'm at in my spiritual walk." So, God has to allow us to go through some things that don't feel good, because we've become barren, fruitless and fallow or empty. I'm reminded of an old song that the Winans used to sing, "Break up that fallow ground." Fallow ground is ground that's been left idle and it becomes dry and hard, filled with weeds. Every spring before my grandfather planted his garden, he had to first break up the ground with a plow to turn the soil and break it up because it had been sitting idle throughout the winter.

Sometimes we're broken and it doesn't feel good, and it stinks. We must come out of complacency so that we can grow. The gardener said, "give it a year". In other words, it's going to take some time. God has an appointed time for everything He wants to give you and do through you. 'The Wait' is not in vain.

You may say, "I pay my tithes and offerings." But God is saying, "Wait." "I fast and pray and read the Word." But God is saying, "Wait." " I clean the church and sing in the choir." But God is saying, "Wait." "I'm doing everything I know to do." But God is still saying, "Wait."

You see you can't make yourself happy. Making you happy is God's job. And if He's not in it, it's counterfeit. However, having joy is up to you, and you do that by praying, staying in the Word, and not worrying. When we move ahead of God trying to obtain something, feeling like we deserve it, we instead become selfish and self-centered. Sure, you could do it, and the Lord may bless it, but it won't be as blessed as if you would just simply wait on Him. Psalm 127:1a says, "Except the LORD build the house, they labouin vain that build it." The bottom line is you can't bless you like God can bless you.

Sometimes it gets so hard to wait and just rest in God. Psalm 23:3a says, "He restores my soul…" The root word for restore is 'rest'. With restoration comes rest. My soul is resting in the Lord. Stay in God's will and be blessed. Get out of God's will and be cursed. Hebrews 10:36 says, "For ye have need of patience, that, after ye have done the will of God, ye might receive the promise."

When we see everybody else being blessed and not us, we become impatient and take matters into our own hands. Then, before you know it, we've made a mess of things. But when God does it, it's perfect. One thing I've learned is that my life didn't turn out the way I thought it would. But it's not over yet. Life will bring changes, physically, mentally, spiritually.

My mother once said, "You have to get used to a *new normal*." When things happen that knock you off your feet, you have to adjust to a new way of doing things, a new way of life. You can't let *what if* come in or it will depress you. You have to tell yourself to enjoy the here and now. Psalm 32:8 (New Living Translation) says, "The LORD says, "I will guide you along the best pathway for your life. I will advise you and watch over you." The word 'trust' means, "to have or place confidence in as being dependable or reliable; to count on; to hope or expect." When we trust God, place our confidence in Him, count on Him, and expect Him to do what we ask, we are eternally blessed.

Don't Forget

Be sober, be vigilant; because your adversary the devil, as a roaring lion, walketh about seeking whom he may devour.

(1 Peter 5:8)

The devil wants you defeated. He has stolen some things from you, your peace, your joy, your anointing, your marriage, your children, your home. But now we're getting ready to snatch victory from defeat. Matthew 11:12 says, "The kingdom of heaven suffereth violence, and the violent take it by force." You have the favor of God. He's proven His favor over and over in His Word.

He proved it to Joseph. Even though he lived in a dysfunctional home, that consisted of having a father who had four different wives. If that's not a recipe for dysfunction, I don't know what is. He was hated by his brothers, so much so, that they put him in a pit just so that they can come back later and kill him, but decided to sell him as a slave instead. He was taken to a foreign land to live with people he didn't know. A while later, he was put in prison for being accused of rape. Two of the king's servants ended up in his jail cell. They both had a dream that Joseph interpreted for them. One of them received a death sentence and the other one returned to his position in the king's palace. But before his release, he promised Joseph that he would mention him to the king upon his release, about how he met this guy is prison who had the ability to interpret dreams. But wouldn't you know it, he forgot all about Joseph. But because we serve a faithful God, Joseph was later remembered by his cellmate and became the most powerful man in Egypt after Pharaoh.

Then, there was Job, the wealthiest and most influential man in his land, until he lost everything he had, became bankrupt and lost all ten of his children in a tornado of some sort. And on top of all that, his wife tells him to curse God and die. It was tragedy after tragedy. But in the last chapter of the book, Job received twice as many animals as he had before. He had ten more sons and daughters, which the Bible says of his daughters, "There were no women as beautiful as the daughters of Job...The Lord blessed the latter end of Job more than his beginning." He received longevity. He lived to see his sons' sons down to the fourth generation. He died "old and full of days."

Then there were the three Hebrew boys, Shadrach, Meshach and Abednego in Daniel 3. They had good jobs as they were appointed over the affairs of the province of Babylon. We know the story about how they refused to bow to King Nebuchadnezzar's golden statue and were thrown in the fiery furnace. That goes to show you that position can't keep you. Only God can keep you.

In the chapter before, Daniel interpreted a dream for Nebuchadnezzar. He was so amazed at this gift that Daniel possessed that he proclaimed, "Of a truth it is, that your God is a God of gods, and a Lord of kings, and a revealer of secrets..." But right before he throws Shadrach, Meshach and Abednego in the fiery furnace, he denies God saying, "...and who is that God that shall deliver you out of my hands?" How quickly we forget. How quickly we forget who God really is. After the Lord brings us through one test with the victory, here comes another one, and we're worrying again just like we did the last time.

If the Lord blessed you to pay your bills last

month, though money was tight and you didn't see any extra money in your near future, won't He also give you the resources you need to pay your bills this month? Then, why are you worried? If He brought you through the first time, don't you know that He will bring you out again and again and again? If God be for you, He's more than the world against you. Hold your peace and let the Lord fight your battles.

Take a lesson from Shadrach, Meshach and Abednego and remain steadfast and unmovable. Don't be shaken! Make up in your mind that you will have NO FEAR. Don't waver. The Hebrew boys had no doubt. "If it be so, our God whom we serve is able to deliver us from the burning fiery furnace, and he will deliver us out of thine hand, O king. But if not, be it known unto thee, O king, that we will not serve thy gods, nor worship the golden image which thou hast set up." Their faith was in God. Growing up, they heard the stories about how God delivered the Israelites from Pharaoh's hand and miraculously parted the Red Sea so they could cross on dry ground and not drown. They didn't forget. Isaiah 43:2 says, "When you pass through the waters, I will be with you; and when you pass through the rivers, they will not sweep over you. When you walk through the fire, you will not be burned; the flames will not set you ablaze." (NIV)

Daniel 3:19 says, "Then was Nebuchadnezzar full of fury, and the form of his visage was changed against Shadrach, Meshach, and Abednego: therefore he spake, and commanded that they should heat the furnace one seven times more than it was wont to be heated." Nebuchadnezzar's countenance changed. You see, people aren't always going to understand why you act the way you do, how you can have such peace and not have a care in the world. So Nebuchadnezzar is like, "What? Do you know who I am? You can't talk to me like that. Who do you think you are?" See, now he's mad because he's never, in all his life, heard men talk to him with such boldness and courage. He was so angry that he ordered the fire to be turned up seven times more than normal.

Sometimes, before your situation gets better, it gets worse. Sometimes, the Lord allows the fire to be turned up in our lives, not so we'll be burned out and just so tired that we're no good for anything and we just want to give up and die. No. God is not trying to beat you down, but He wants to build you up. But sometimes the fire has to be turned up for the increase of the miracle, for your good and His glory. It's one thing when you need healing from a headache, but it's a whole other thing when you need healing from cancer. It's one thing to have a $100 need, but it's another to have a $10,000 need.

God is saying, "I know it looks bad right now, and it seems as if it's gone from bad to worse, but hold on, because I'm not through with you yet!" That house you've been believing God for, it's coming. That job, husband, wife, promotion, raise, car, anointing, deliverance from addiction— whatever you desire, you must stand on the Word of God, believing, and it will come to past!

As we read the rest of Daniel 3, we see that God delivers them from the fiery furnace. Sometimes, your blessing is on the other side of the fire. For some of us, as soon as we felt the heat from the furnace, we would've been bowing down. We would've given up saying, "It's not worth it." Ephesians 6:13 says, "Wherefore take unto you the whole armor of God, that ye may be able to withstand in the evil day, and having done all, to stand." Shadrach, Meshach and Abednego weren't afraid because they had their armor on. Do you have your armor on? When we walk in obedience to God's Word, we walk in victory, no matter what it looks like on the outside.

God wants our best, not just any old thing, in everything we do, in word and deed. Sometimes we have to go through the fire, but because of God's grace, we won't be burned.

In the old testament, the Israelites would offer animal sacrifices and offerings that the priest would burn on the altar. Leviticus 3:16 says, "And the priest shall burn them upon the altar: it is the food of the offering made by fire for a *sweet savor*." He allows us to go through the fire, tests and trials, but when we offer unto Him the sacrifice of praise, the fruit of our lips giving thanks, it's a sweet-smelling savor to Him. He reconciles us to Himself. He draws us close to Him.

I Never Would've Thought

It is good for me that I have been afflicted; that I might learn thy statutes.

(Psalm 199:71)

Have you ever been through such a severe test that you thought, "I never would've thought?" One week I had three different conversations with three different family members. Each of them told me about a test they were going through. Alhough these three women were experiencing three different situations, the one thing that these women said to me was, "I never would've thought."

Many of us have said or thought these four

words at least once during our lives. Or maybe you didn't say, "I never would've thought." Maybe you said, "I can't believe this is happening to me." You may have said, "I pay my tithes. I come to church. I get up early in the morning to pray and read my Bible. I fast. Please Lord, not me! I praise you more than anybody."

In the book Ruth we read about a woman whose name was Naomi. She was married with two sons. There was a famine in the land, so her husband decided that they would relocate to a more prosperous land. While there, her sons found companions and got married. However, later on, things took a turn for the worst. Naomi's husband and both of her sons passed away. She no longer had any men left to take care of her. She only had her two daughters-in-law, Orpah and Ruth.

Naomi felt sorry for herself. Here she was, with no support, no 401k, no retirement, and no pension. I'm sure that Naomi probably thought to herself once or twice, "I never would've thought."

Look at David. He was anointed to be a king. But first, he had to live as a vagabond, was running for his life from King Saul and hiding in caves. I'm sure that he probably thought to himself, "I never would've thought."

With everything I've been through and have experienced in my life, I have come to know a peace, contentment and courage like I've never known before. Hebrews 2:10 says that Jesus was made perfect through his sufferings. When we are weak, then are we strong. God will turn your *'I never would've thoughts'* around. He's going to bring you to the place that you'll say, "I never would've thought I would have so much peace and so much joy! I never would've thought I'd be so blessed and anointed!"

Matthew 7:25 says, "And the rain descended, and the floods came, and the winds blew, and beat upon that house; and it fell not: for it was founded upon a rock." The storms will come in your life. The floods will come and the winds are going to blow and try to beat you down. The devil will try to beat your marriage down, your finances, your family, and your health.

At the risk of making this sound like a children's book, I can't help but think about the fable of the three little pigs. I won't tell the whole story, but just for a moment, picture the "big, bad wolf" as the devil. He sure knows how to show his fangs and huff and puff until he gets us to give up.

Sometimes we're faced with circumstances that leave us feeling like we're in a whirlwind, or a spiritual tsunami. That's why it's vital that you build your house. When I say house, I mean your spirit and soul. You must build yourself up on the word of God. Jesus is our Rock.

The songwriter says, "On Christ the solid rock I stand. All other ground is sinking sand." As long as you're standing on the word, the Rock of Jesus Christ, you won't fall. The rain may fall, the floods may come, and the winds may blow. But Isaiah 59:19b says, "When the enemy shall come in like a flood, the Spirit of the LORD shall lift up a standard against him."

Declare to the enemy, "I'm taking my husband back! I'm taking my wife back! I'm taking my children back! I'm taking my health back! I'm taking my finances back!"

Seasons Change

To everything there is a season, and a time to every purpose under the heaven.

(Ecclesiastes 3:1)

As I was driving home one day, I was driving over some potholes, thinking to myself, "I'm tired of these potholes. Why are they here? Winter is over!" At that moment, I felt the Lord said to me, "Your winter is over. I'm getting ready to bring you into your spring season."

In the winter, the weather is bad. It's cold. There are dangerous driving conditions with sleet and ice on the road. There are blizzards in the winter. The outside looks gray. Everything is barren, and there are more accidents in the winter. And of course, if you're not properly dressed, it is possible to die in the winter if you stay outside long enough.

The same applies spiritually. If you don't have your armor on, the enemy will defeat you. However, there's beauty in every season.

In the winter, the snow is beautiful. Have you ever seen ice on branches on a cold winter morning? It looks absolutely breathtaking at times. We also celebrate Christmas in the winter, which is the most celebrated holiday of the year. Everybody loves Christmas.

What I'm trying to say is, every season, even winter, has beauty in it. And the same applies to our lives. We're going to go through different seasons in our lives. Some good, and some bad. But behind every dark cloud is a silver lining. Romans 8:28 says, "And we know that all things work together for good to them that love God, to them who are the called according to his purpose."

We will experience barrenness, or droughts, in life. Drought is the opposite of abundance. During our winter seasons, the Lord will provide us with just enough to sustain us. You can rest assured that while you're going through, the Lord will sustain you. To sustain means to 'keep alive; supply with needed nourishment; encourage to keep going; to provide endurance'. Winter is only for a short season, though it seems long at times.

Then comes Spring. Spring is indicative of new life. The trees and flowers begin to blossom and vibrant color is coming back on the scene. It's a new morning!

Psalm 30:5 says, "For his anger endures but a moment; in his favor is life: weeping may endure for a night, but joy comes in the morning."

One day I was curious about the meaning of the word *spring*, not the season, but an actual spring, like a bed spring. According to website *madehow.com*, "a spring is a device that changes its shape in response to an *external force*, returning to its original shape when the force is removed."

During our *winter* seasons of life, we may find ourselves bent over from the external forces or pressures we find ourselves under. Your external forces may be people putting their mouths on you, illness, financial burdens, marital issues, or even mental problems. But one thing you must remember is even though a spring may be pulled and stretched, once that external force is removed, it resumes its original shape.

Isaiah 43:19 says, "Behold, I will do a new thing; now it shall *spring* forth; shall ye not know it? I will even make a way in the wilderness, and rivers in the desert (drought)." You may be experiencing some difficult situations that are causing you to be stretched, or pulled in this direction and that direction. Rest assured, your spring is coming in its appointed time. Notice that each season only lasts for a few months. In other words, trouble doesn't last always.

We will go through different seasons in our lives. It's inevitable. But rest assured that the Lord will deliver you through each and every one of them.

Transformers

And Jesus said unto them, Because of your unbelief: for verily I say unto you, If ye have faith as a grain of mustard seed, ye shall say unto this mountain, Remove hence to yonder place; and it shall remove; and nothing shall be impossible unto you.

(Matthew 17:20)

In 2007 the movie, "Transformers", came out on DVD. As I watched it, the Lord gave me revelation on the different characters, their names and what they meant. I remember the names of the three of them in particular, Devastator, Bone Crusher and Blackout. Devastator had the power to bring devastation.

Bone Crusher had the power to crush. And Blackout had the power to bring darkness.

Devastate means, "to lay waste; ruin." Crush means, "to press, squeeze, or bear down with great force as to break; to quiet or bring under control." And then a blackout consists of darkness, no light. These words describe some of the devil's characteristics. He brings opposition to devastate you, to ruin your peace and your joy. Then, he tries to crush us by bringing trouble. He uses troubles and problems to squeeze the life out of you, to break you and to bring you under his control. Then, his most famous tactic is to bring darkness by getting you to focus on your problem and forget about the power you have and the power of our great and awesome God. He's good at making us lose hope until we see no light at the end of the tunnel.

You are a child of God, and with your position comes privileges. However, responsibility to use the commanding power that has been delegated to you comes with your position, also. Read what the Bible says belongs to you. Then, command the devil to release it and let it go! Luke 17:6 says, "And the Lord said, If ye had faith as a grain of mustard seed, ye might say unto this sycamine tree, Be thou plucked up by the root, and be thou planted in the sea; and it should obey you."

When we begin to call those things which be

not as though they were, and be fully persuaded that what He has promised He is well able to perform, God will send His angels to go forth and bring to you all that belongs to you. You have the power to bring life to your dead situations.

In John 11 we see that Lazarus, Jesus' friend, had died. He had been dead for four days by the time Jesus arrived on the scene. By time Jesus got there, rigor mortis had already begun to set in. But as far as Jesus was concerned, that didn't even matter. Even though he had already been dead long enough for his body to decay and become putrid, it didn't matter to Jesus. He spoke to Lazarus' dead body and commanded it to "Come Forth!" Every muscle, bone and fiber in his body had no choice, but to rise up and obey.

If Jesus can bring life to a dead body, surely you have the power to bring life to your dead situation, and watch God turn it around!

It's Time To Worship

And at midnight Paul and Silas prayed, and sang praises unto God: and the prisoners heard them. And suddenly there was a great earthquake, so that the foundations of the prison were shaken and immediately all the doors were opened, and every one's bands were loosed.

(Acts 16:25)

We know the story of Paul of Silas in Acts 16. They were put in prison for casting a demon out of a fortune teller. But they didn't let their circumstances stop their praise. Each of us has a *suddenly*. And when it happens, you won't be able to say, "Look what I did," but instead you will say, "Look what the Lord has done!"

In the midst of your storm, you should make yourself a sanctuary. A sanctuary is a consecrated place, a place for praise and worship, a place of refuge and protection. Get yourself a room in your home that you can get alone with God, a place where you can be intimate with Him. That's what God is seeking, intimacy.

I heard someone break down the word 'intimacy' like this: 'In-to-me- see'. This is a place where Daddy God can fill you with his love and his wisdom; a place for you to cry out to him with no inhibition. He longs for your worship, not for what He can do, but because of who He is. He likes to be pursued. Praise is when you thank God for what He's done. Worship is when you thank God for who He is. "If I don't have a car, house, husband, etc., I worship you Lord because of who you are—just because you're God."

When you worship God correctly, the blessings will come. You receive strength. Nehemiah 8:10 says, "...the joy of the Lord is your strength." Demons feel uncomfortable with praise directed towards God, and they will not remain in a place where they don't feel comfortable. And not only that, but it confuses the enemy. Psalm 8:2 says, "Out of the mouth of babes and sucklings hast thou ordained strength because of thine enemies, that thou mightest still the enemy and the avenger." In II Chronicles 20, the Moabites and the Ammonites came to fight against King Jehoshaphat and the people of Judah. The king commanded the people to set their faces to fast and seek God for guidance. And the Lord answered in a powerful way:

Ye shall not need to fight in this battle: set yourselves, stand ye still, and see the salvation of the LORD with you, O Judah and Jerusalem: fear not, nor be dismayed; tomorrow go out against them: for the LORD will be with you. And Jehoshaphat bowed his head with his face to the ground: and all Judah and the inhabitants of Jerusalem fell before the LORD, worshipping the LORD. And the Levites, of the children of the Kohathites, and of the children of the Korhites, stood up to praise the LORD God of Israel with a loud voice on high. And they rose early in the morning, and went forth into the wilderness of Tekoa: and as they went forth, Jehoshaphat stood and said, Hear me, O Judah, and ye inhabitants of Jerusalem; Believe in the LORD your God, so shall ye be established; believe his prophets, so shall ye prosper. And when he had consulted with the people, he appointed singers unto the LORD, and that should praise the beauty of holiness, as they went out before the army, and to say, Praise the LORD; for his mercy endureth for ever. And when they began to sing and to praise, the LORD set ambushments against the children of Ammon, Moab, and mount Seir, which were come against Judah; and they were smitten. For the children of Ammon and Moab stood up against the inhabitants of mount Seir, utterly to slay and destroy them: and when they had made an end of the inhabitants of Seir, every one helped to destroy another. And when Judah came toward the watch tower in the wilderness, they looked unto the multitude, and, behold, they were dead bodies fallen to the earth, and none escaped. And when Jehoshaphat and his people came to take away the spoil of them, they found among them in abundance both riches with the dead bodies, and precious jewels, which they stripped off for themselves, more than they could carry away: and they were three days in gathering of the spoil, it was so much. (II Chronicles 20:17-25)

God is getting to enlarge your territories and open doors for you that no man can shut. We go through various tests and the first one we want to blame is the devil. Joel 2:25 says, "And I will restore to you the years that the locust hath eaten, the cankerworm, and the caterpillar, and the palmerworm, my great army which *I* sent among you." God sent the cankerworm, caterpillar and the palmerworm. Satan can't do anything to you except God permits it.

Let's look at Job. In the first chapter we see Satan, "Now there was a day when the sons of God came to present themselves before the LORD, and Satan came also among them. And the LORD said unto Satan, Hast thou considered my servant Job, that there is none like him in the earth, a perfect and an upright man, one that fears God, and eschews evil?" (Job 1:6,8)

Notice that the Lord mentioned Job's name, not Satan. Satan made the statement that because the Lord had blessed Job so much, of course he was perfect and upright, because he had a "hedge about him". Then, the Lord gave Satan permission to touch everything Job had, including his children. After all that, we find Satan standing before the Lord again for a second time in chapter two. And the Lord says the same thing He said earlier. And again Satan, the 'accuser of the brethren', says in verse four, "Skin for skin, yea, all that a man hath will he give for his life." So, the Lord gave him permission to afflict his body, but he couldn't take his life. But as stated earlier, God restored everything back to Job—double.

Everything you're going through is no surprise to God. But you must answer the question, "Will you break and give up, or will you worship?" He's calling you. God loves you so much. He leaves it up to you if you will love Him back or not. Are you willing to get quiet before the Lord, turn off the television and the computer, get off the phone and find yourself a secret place? When you worship, He'll give you peace, joy, anointing, power, solutions to problems, and the list goes on. God wants to talk to you. Are you listening? He wants to have first place in your life. When we don't put Him first, we keep ourselves from receiving the fullness of His blessings.

When you pray and worship and believe God's word, that's your part. If you'll do that, God will back you. He'll have your back. And when God has your back, everything else either has to get in line or get out of the way.

Bonus Chapter

And the Lord restored the fortunes of Job, when he had prayed for his friends. And the Lord gave Job twice as much as he had before.

(Job 42:10)

I wrote this book seven years ago in 2010, but it didn't contain this final chapter that you are now reading.

Seven years ago, Albert was in prison as stated in the beginning. He came home five years ago on February 8, 2012. He wasn't supposed to come home until May 2016. God gave us favor and allowed him to come home four years earlier. However, the few weeks before his release were the hardest for me, more than any other time during the 12 years he was gone.

Bonus Chapter

I remember it like it was yesterday. It was New Year's Eve 2011. We just knew, I mean we were so sure that Albert would've been home by now—but it hadn't happened.

I was talking to Albert on the phone, crying and telling him how I don't know if I could wait any longer for him. I had gotten to the end of my rope. I was absolutely tired of waiting. He did his best to encourage me, but it didn't work. I was done—or so I thought.

New Year's Day 2012 had come and gone. Less than a week later, I got a phone call from a close friend of ours who we used to go to church with. She had been writing letters to the judge to plea for Albert's release. God used her to fight for Albert in ways that I can't begin to describe. She was our advocate. She literally went to bat for us and without her, I know that Albert wouldn't be home with me today.

She called me while I was at work. She told me the best news that I have heard to date—that the judge was going to see Albert. That's all we needed to know. We knew that our time had come. We knew that the judge wouldn't take the time or go through the trouble to have Albert transported three hours from where he was, unless he was going to let him come home.

God has an amazing sense of humor. I

couldn't believe it! Just when I was on the verge of giving up, God finally answered our prayer. My husband was coming home.

The kids and I drove to the courthouse in Toledo, filled with anticipation. The judge even told him that he could leave Ohio and go to Michigan to live with his family. So, for the first six weeks he was home, life was glorious—until.

Albert got a phone call from his parole officer letting him know that he had 48 hours to leave the state of Michigan and return back to Ohio to live. Although the judge released him to go to Michigan, Michigan wasn't having it.

We were living in a beautiful apartment in a beautiful neighborhood, within walking distance from the park and downtown. I had a good job and the kids loved their schools and their friends. If Albert had to leave, that meant that our kids and I would have to leave, too. Needless to say, we didn't want to leave. So, we went to the parole officer in Michigan to try to plea our case.

He was rude, to say the least, and could care less. We were sad and angry. It would take time for us to find a place to live in Toledo and we didn't want to take the kids out of school in the middle of the school year. So Albert went back to Toledo alone.

He was able to find temporary housing.

But, again we found ourselves separated from each other, only able to see each other on the weekends.

In the meantime, we were determined to be together and not let anything else keep us apart from each other. We paid off my credit card debts and borrowed money from a friend for a down payment for a home. Five months later, we were together again, this time for good.

The Lord has blessed us both with good jobs. We live in a beautiful home and we both serve in the ministry at our church.

There's a paragraph I wrote earlier in in which I was talking about how I couldn't sing for a while and use the talents that God had given, but that He reassured me that I would sing again and that His anointing would be upon me. I almost took that part out of this edition of the book, but I felt to leave it in.

Today, I now serve as the worship leader at my church. When I sing, I sometimes look out at the audience, and I can see tears strolling down people's faces. I know that it's not because I sound bad, but it's God's promise coming to past. What He promised me more than 17 years ago has come to past. People come to me often to tell me how they're blessed by my ministry. I know that because of everything I've been through, during that barren, dry and hard season of my life, God was equipping me to walk in the power and authority that I now possess.

Earlier in this chapter, I mentioned how I was at the end of my rope and I really didn't think that I could keep waiting so patiently. And then, BAM, our prayer was answered.

Isn't it funny sometimes how that just when you're about to give up, here comes God to the rescue, like a knight in shining armor. He may not come when we want Him, but He's always on time.

Whatever it is you've been praying and asking God for, don't give up. You may find yourself in a storm right now, and it seems like it's taking God forever—don't give up. Know that He is with you in the midst of your storm.

I made it. That's how I know that *you* can, and WILL make it as will. My storm lasted twelve years. It was a long winter season, but my spring has come—and yours will, too.

God has given me this new saying, "I'm ready for my NEXT." I don't know what my *next* is, but I know it's going to be awesome.

What you're facing right now won't last forever. He is preparing you for your next. Stay in the process. You've come this far, so you might as well stay in it until God finally says, "It's over.

Now walk into your next season." I promise you that your next is filled with blessings that are going to blow your mind!

Made in the USA
Lexington, KY
24 October 2017